CONFUCIUS IN 90 MINUTES

Confucius
IN 90 MINUTES

Paul Strathern

IVAN R. DEE
CHICAGO

Library of Congress Cataloging-in-Publication Data:
Strathern, Paul, 1940–
    Confucius in 90 minutes / Paul Strathern
        p.   cm. — (Philosophers in 90 minutes)
    Includes bibliographical references and index.
    ISBN 1-56663-237-4 (alk. paper). — ISBN 1-56663-238-2
    (paper : alk. paper)
    1. Confucius.   2. Philosophy, Confucian.   I. Title.
II. Series.
B128.C8S8   1999
181'.112—dc21   98-52666

Contents

CONFUCIUS IN 90 MINUTES

Introduction

Confucius knew all about life, but we know very little about his life. This leaves us at rather a loss when judging him personally. He told us how to behave, but we can't find out precisely what he was up to.

Confucius is a close contender for The Most Influential Man in History—so we're lucky that his philosophy was nebulous and rather boring. His collection of well-meaning platitudes, quaint maxims, and quasi-enigmatic anecdotes combined to produce an ideal philosophy for civil servants. And this was precisely Confucius's intention. Unlike other sages, he had no wish to see his disciples become penniless vagabonds

7

roaming the highways and byways in a state of unemployable enlightenment. His aim was to turn his pupils into good government officials, and in this he succeeded beyond his wildest expectations. For more than two thousand years his teaching provided rules of conduct and spiritual fodder for the clerks, schoolmasters, ministers, and administrators amidst the stultifying conformity of the Chinese Empire. This was the empire that gave us the curse: "May you live in interesting times." In Confucian China, boredom was bliss. Not surprising when you consider the alternatives. If you stepped out of line, committing even a minor offense, you were lucky if you got away with castration. The court of many an irascible Chinese ruler sounded as if it was run by a bevy of schoolchildren.

Until the Communist revolution of 1949, Confucianism was almost synonymous with the Chinese way of life. During the Mao era in mainland China, Confucianism was regarded with deep ambivalence. Confucius himself was reviled as one of the class of "landlords and capitalists." (In fact, he qualified for neither of these

8

exalted categories. Confucius spent most of his life unemployed, was always short of money, and had no estate.) During the Cultural Revolution of the 1960s, the Red Guards attempted to purge the last remnants of Confucianism from Chinese thought. Even so, Chairman Mao continued on occasion to encourage his comrades with sayings by Confucius. Both of these latter facts point to a strong undercurrent of Confucianism in Chinese thought which persisted beneath the veneer of Marxism.

On the other hand, Confucianism remained, and remains, very much alive throughout the Chinese diaspora—from Taiwan to Chinatowns the world over. The sayings of Confucius succeed from one generation to the next, his name having achieved a cultural centrality similar to Shakespeare for the English or Goethe for the Germans.

Yet surprisingly, Confucius himself was a failure. Or so he thought (and who are we to contradict such a wise man). Confucius considered that he had not succeeded in life, and died a disappointed man.

Confucius's Life and Works

Confucius is the latinized form of Kungfutzu (which means "the master Kung"). He was born in the sixth century B.C. and lived for the most part in the north-central coastal region of China. The sixth century B.C. was arguably the most significant in human evolution since the first caveman inadvertently set fire to his home. Beside witnessing the birth of Confucius, this century also saw the founding of Taoism, the birth of Buddha, and the inception of Greek philosophy. Why these vital intellectual events should have taken place just then, for the most part in civilizations that were in disparate states of development and had no contact with each other,

11

remains a mystery. (Some of the solutions put forward—visits from alien spaceships, exceptional activity on the surface of the sun, brain disease, etc.—would suggest that our mental development has not progressed much since this era.)

Confucius was born in 551 B.C. in the feudal state of Lu, which now forms part of the north-central coastal province of Shantung. He came from a long line of impoverished nobility and is said to have been directly descended from the rulers of the Shang dynasty.

This was China's earliest dynasty, which lasted more than six hundred years from the eighteenth to the twelfth century B.C. It was said that the people produced azure pots painted with beautiful flowers and used pink cowrie shells as currency. According to legend, its inhabitants were credited with inventing Chinese writing so that they could communicate with their ancestors by means of messages carved on tortoise shells. Naturally such enchanting nonsense was dismissed by serious historians, until recent archaeological discoveries confirmed the

12

existence and lifestyle of just such a dynasty during the second millennium B.C. But unfortunately no messages to early members of Confucius's family have yet been discovered among the tortoiseshell tomes.

What we do know is that Confucius's father was a minor military official and was seventy at the time of Confucius's birth. When Confucius was three his father died and he was brought up by his mother. (Curiously, of the dozen or so figures who founded the world's great philosophies and religions, a large majority were brought up in single-parent families.)

Late in life, Confucius was to remember: "When I was fifteen I was only interested in studying." This was the bedrock of his life, which he would later see as having been divided into distinct stages: "... When I was thirty I began my life; at forty I was self-assured; at fifty I understood my place in the vast scheme of things; at sixty I learned to give up arguing; and now at seventy I can do whatever I like without disrupting my life." How much of this is genuine spiritual autobiography, and how much is Confucius's variant on traditional wisdom concerning the "ages of man," it's difficult to say. Either way, it contains little of personal particularity—or what the modern reader would consider a "life."

Apart from Confucius's self-proclaimed love of learning, little is known of his early years. Little, that is, apart from the usual collection of unlikely stories that accumulate around any such transcendent figure (birds charmed from the trees, an uncle's favorite dog brought back to life, comets, etc.). By now the six-hundred-year-old Chou dynasty, which had brought civilization to China, was beginning to fall apart. This was a feudal period, with vassal city states switching allegiances and going to war almost at will. The warlords lived as warlords have always lived (massacre, famine, orgy), and the rest of the population merely made up the numbers so that their masters would not be reduced to less populous activities (murder, starvation, depravity).

Human misery was rife, on the traditional oriental scale—not witnessed since the Communist revolution, which nonetheless managed to retain a few of the traditional miseries. This grounding in everyday horrors had a profound effect upon young Confucius. It was to give a toughness and practicality to his thinking, which it seldom lost. Confucius quickly saw that if such untold suffering was to cease, the whole notion of society would have to change. A society ought to work for the benefit of all its members rather than be used merely as a pretext for the excesses of its rulers. Confucius was the first to formulate this oft-ignored cliché. Not until two hundred years later did the ancient Greeks start discussing this point. But because they *discussed* it, they quickly developed a sophisticated abstract notion of justice. Confucius didn't have the opportunity to discuss such matters during his formative years, so his thoughts remained practical. He decided that the notion of society would have to change, but not society itself. The ruler must rule and the administrator carry out his duties, as surely as the father must be a father to his son. The revolution he eventually taught was one of attitude and behavior. We

15

must each strive to fulfill our role as virtuously as possible.

But Confucius did make pronouncements on this and related subjects which allowed his followers much room for interpretation. For example: "If a theory spreads, it is because heaven wills it." "It is difficult to be a ruler, yet it is not easy to be a subject either." "Men of integrity do things differently." "Not to act when justice commands, is cowardice."

This wide, quasi-cohesive *lack* of logic that characterized Confucius's teaching was to prove Confucianism's great strength. In the end you could never prove it entirely wrong, and if you looked hard enough you could find something in it to prove almost anything right. Confucianism was to share this strength with the Bible as well as the sacred texts of most lasting creeds.

At eighteen Confucius married and had a son called Lieu, which means "large carp." (Lieu was to prove a disappointment to his illustrious father, and never became the big fish Confucius had hoped for.) Confucius was poor, and to make ends meet he took on a number of jobs, including clerk in a granary store and zookeeper to a menagerie of sacred animals. In his spare time he studied history, music, and liturgy, quickly gaining a reputation as the most learned man in Lu. Confucius was ambitious. He hoped to achieve a high position in the administration so that he could put his ideas into practice. Not surprisingly, the fun-loving rulers had no wish to employ such a spoilsport to run their domains, and Confucius's applications never got beyond the interview stage. (Confucius was an earnest young man who believed in sharing his vast learning with the world: not a great technique for job interviews.) Then, as now, people who couldn't get a job in their chosen field often ended up teaching it. The state of Lu boasted a number of schools teaching court etiquette and ritual to prospective courtiers. These schools were usually staffed by former courtiers who had an expert knowledge of intricate court observances but had lost their job owing to some inadvertent gaffe—which may also have caused them to lose some intimate possessions even more valued than their salary. Confucius decided to set up a school with a difference: he would instruct political administrators on how to rule.

Fortunately Confucius had an engaging and inspiring personality: no questions were asked about his qualifications, and he soon began attracting pupils. His school appears to have been very similar to those developed by the ancient Greek philosophers during the following centuries. The atmosphere was informal. The master conversed with his pupils, sometimes on foot, sometimes sitting under the shade of a tree. Occasionally the master would deliver a set-piece lecture, but mostly lessons consisted of question-and-answer sessions.

The master's replies were often in the form of homilies. "If you lead an untrained army into battle, you throw it away." "The superior man is sparing in words, but not in deeds." "If you don't change your faults, you become even more faulty." These remarks must have appeared almost as banal 2,500 years ago as they do today. Yet we are told that Confucius didn't suffer fools gladly. "If I indicate one corner of a subject, and the pupil cannot work out the other three for himself, I send him away." There was no room for poltroons or polygons in Confucius's school. He usually had about two dozen pupils, ranging from princes to paupers. The sayings of Confucius that have come down to us are not all banal—some are contentious, others opaque or enigmatic, and a number are profound. ("Anyone who does not know the value of words will never understand men." "The full life seeks what is in itself, the empty life seeks what appears in others.") His remarks are said to contain the occasional bit of quiet oriental humor, but this remains beyond the sonic range of most occidental ears.

Confucius was essentially a moral teacher. He was always sincere and distrusted eloquence. His aim was to teach his pupils how to behave properly. If they wished to rule people, they must first learn how to rule themselves. But the very core of his teaching has a familiar ring: virtue means to love one another. This, humanity's most profound moral sentiment, was articulated by Confucius more than five hundred years before the birth of Christ. Yet it was not intended as a religious principle. Confucius may have founded a religion (Confucianism), but his teachings were not religious *per se*. Nor, in fact, was his religion—and this Chinese puzzle has certainly contributed to its longevity.

There is yet another twist to this paradox. Confucius's teachings may not have been religious, but he himself was. Or appeared to be. Mostly. On other occasions he was evasive. His sayings on this matter range from the fulsome to the enigmatic. How much either of these attitudes was dictated by expediency or political necessity we will never know.

Confucius appears to have believed that the universe contains a power for the good—which some may regard as faith of the highest order, there being no observed evidence whatsoever to support such optimism. Confucius praised the virtuous man who lived in awe of heaven, but he considered most religious practices of his age to be superstitious nonsense. On the other hand, he delighted in ritual and saw its effects as highly beneficial.

In this, as in much else, Confucius bears a

striking resemblance to Socrates. Indeed, more than one great orientalist has likened Confucius to a Socratic Christ. (As well as vilifying three of history's greatest figures, this flabby calumny contains the usual irritating pearl of truth.)

The key element of Confucius's teachings was symbolized by the Chinese character *jen*. This stood for a conceptual blend of magnanimity, virtue, and love of humanity. It bears a close proximity to the Christian notion of compassion and loving-kindness. (*Jen* is also said to have put the Zen into Zen Buddhism, though this took place several centuries after the death of Confucius.) Along with *jen*, Confucius's teachings stress the complementary qualities of *te* (virtue) and *yi* (righteousness). In everyday life he stressed the need for *li* (decorum) and observance of traditional rites. But observance had to be a meaningful participation; when it became mere formality this reflected a spiritual malaise, both in the individual and in the community. Confucius's aim was to produce Chuntzu (superior individuals) who would live a life of harmony and virtue, free from anxiety and distress.

21

Having said this, it's worth noting that Confucius's central notion of *jen* has given rise to a wide variety of interpretations. The word itself has been translated as anything from moral perfection to magnanimity, from humaneness to compassion, or even simple altruism.

The Chinese character for *jen* is made up of two elements, that for "man" and that for "two." Man + two = man-to-manness. In other words, *jen* is not concerned with individual spiritual morality, more with social behavior, or moral character demonstrated in a public setting. Confucius makes this plain in his sayings (or *Lun Yu*, frequently referred to as the Analects). "When asked the meaning of *jen*, Confucius replied: 'It means to love your fellow human beings.'" Later he elaborates on this: "There are five things, and whoever manages to put these into practice is *jen*. [These are] respectfulness, tolerance, trustworthiness, quick-witted diligence, and generosity. If a man is respectful he will not be treated with insolence. If he is tolerant he will win over the multitude. If he is trustworthy, then others will entrust him with responsibility. If he is diligent and quick-witted he will achieve results. If he is compassionate he will be good enough to be put in command of other men."

Confucius saw *jen* as part of education. In other words, one had to be taught such behavior rather than simply learning it from experience. In his time, education was regarded as a matter of learning how to behave, rather than the acquisition of specific knowledge. Confucius concurred with this attitude. The acquisition of knowledge was wisdom, not *jen*. The latter not only involved morality but also many traditional values, especially filial piety. This was much stronger than simple respect for one's parents, and involved taking on board their entire system of traditional values and rituals.

Already by Confucius's time the traditions of Chinese morality were well developed. The two key concepts were *tao* and *te*. *Tao* literally means "the Way"—in the sense that Christ used the word when he said: "I am the light and the way." A more familiar Western equivalent would be "truth," though this does not contain the progressive element present in *tao*. It was vital for the individual's spiritual well-being that he adhere to the Way. But *tao* didn't apply just to individuals; an entire state might stray from the Way.

Confucius's attitude toward *tao* was highly ambivalent. With gnomic irony he concluded: "He has not lived in vain who dies the day he is told about the Way." Confucius had little time for the religion that grew out of this concept—Taoism. It represented an inwardness that caused the individual to withdraw from society. For Confucius, morality was all about *involvement* in society. On the other hand, he approved of the Way when it referred to traditional moral observances. Ritual could be a great help in learning *jen*.

The other key concept of traditional Chinese morality was *te*. This is usually translated as "virtue" but also derives from the *te* that means "to get." One gets virtue by following the Way. But once again Confucius is ambivalent here. At one point in his travels, when he was being pursued by the notorious Huan T'ui and in danger of his life, Confucius expressed his equanimity as follows: "Heaven gave me virtue. How can Huan T'ui harm me?" This implies that we receive our virtue from "heaven." For the most part, Confucius appears to have taught that we receive from heaven our individual capacity for virtue. This may differ from individual to individual, but it is up to each of us to cultivate whatever moral potential we possess. This should be our major moral concern, and it was the failure to do so that caused Confucius concern. "Failure to cultivate virtue, failure to ponder upon what I have learned, inability to stand up for what I know is right, inability to reform my defects—these are the things that worry me."

Te could also play an exemplary social role. Public order could be maintained either by punishment or by example. "Lead the people by edicts, restrain them by punishment—and they will keep out of trouble but develop no sense of shame. Lead them by virtue, restrain them with ritual—and they will develop a sense of shame and reform themselves by joining together." This looks like optimism of the highest order. And in the context of sixth-century B.C. China—during the troubled period of the Chou dynasty, when the country was ruled by squabbling petty dictators and warlords—such humane advice appears to be sublime lunacy. There was nothing whatsoever to be gained from such a course of action. Ruling made easy? A contented population? What next?

What was significant about his attitude was its sheer originality. *Te* was nothing less than an *evolutionary* step forward. Compassion, nobility, example—these were indeed novelties in a world of primitive savagery. They appeared impossible; their survival would need nothing short of a miracle. But the miracle eventually happened, both in China (with Confucianism) and in the West (with Christianity). Without this humanitarian element emerging from the savagery of internecine struggle, there would have been no humane civilization. (One has only to look at the bloodshed and hideousness of ancient Egyptian and Mayan civilizations, which advanced without this humanitarian element emerging.)

It is difficult to account for this "impossible" evolutionary step in human society, which first became generally articulated by Confucius. What led him to propose this new humanity? We can only guess. With hindsight we can see that it was a way of allowing us to climb out of the mire of barbarism and fulfill our potential as human beings. Did Confucius instinctively realize this?

The answer seems obvious: Confucius must have been inspired to such action by a belief in God—and a benevolent God, at that. Alas, Confucius was at best an agnostic. He was all for the therapy of ritual, but when it came to a belief in God, an afterlife, or metaphysics of any sort, he remained distinctly evasive. "Chi-lu asked how we should serve the spirits of the dead and the gods. The Master said: 'You are not even able to serve man, how could you serve the spirits?'

"'May I ask about death?'

"'You do not even understand life, how can you understand death?'"

Yet Confucius certainly had an unspoken belief in *something*. It was not transcendental, but it served much the same core purpose as any religion. He believed in the moral purpose of humanity. We have a duty to make ourselves better, to become as fully human as possible, and to become better human beings. This was the only meaningful way to live life. There were no rewards in the afterlife for success, or even punishments for failure. The enterprise was to be pursued for its own sake, regardless of the consequences. Here, more than two millennia before Darwin, was a secular religion utterly in accord with evolution. In its own way, this was an expression of the ultimate nobility in humanity— the pursuit of good for its own sake.

Such high-flown sentiment is all very well, but how should we *actually* behave? Confucius was nothing if not practical, and his morality doesn't shirk from prescribing for the exigencies of behavior in day-to-day living. He advises: "Tame the self" and "What you do not wish for yourself, do not impose on others." It was a matter of attitude and consistency: "Conduct your public affairs without resentment; conduct your private affairs without resentment." We should aim to be "without worries and without fear." But how? "If, after self-examination, a

28

man finds he has nothing to reproach himself for, then what has he to worry about, what has he to fear?"

To modern eyes there appears to be just one damning flaw in Confucius's morality. Our morality tends to reflect the egalitarian aspects of our society. So it should come as no surprise that Confucius's morality reflects the primitive, class-ridden nature of Chinese society during the Chou dynasty more than two and a half millennia ago. Confucius saw morality as a matter of class. The people who fulfilled their moral potential became *jen*. These were superior people: members of the ruling class.

Ruling classes have always believed they are superior people, and the ruling classes of sixth-century B.C. China didn't need Confucius to point out this self-evident truth. On the other hand, they didn't expect people to behave as they did. Heaven forbid! "Do as I say, not as I do." Morality has always been beset by the class question. It's easy enough to be good when society is set up for your benefit and protection. But when the rules are not in one's favor, one feels

29

less inclined to be good (a fact reflected in prison populations the world over, throughout history).

Confucius may have appeared a snob here, but in fact his revolutionary notion of morality did attempt to circumvent the class issue. The superior man may have been upper class, yet if you behaved as he did there was no difference between you and him. But there was more to it than that. The superior man exhibited *exemplary* behavior (in the literal sense of the word). The morality of the superior man was an example (or he simply wasn't a superior man). In this way Confucius made his morality universal, applying to all classes in all periods.

Even so, there are remnants of class distinction in some of his more practical moral advice: "Duke Ching of Ch'i asked Confucius about government. Confucius replied: 'Let the ruler be a ruler; the subject a subject; the father a father; the son a son.' The Duke said: 'Excellent! Indeed, if the ruler is not a ruler, the subject not a subject, the father not a father, the son not a son, I could rely on nothing any more—I wouldn't even know where my next meal was coming from.'" Some have detected an element of irony in Confucius's sayings, noting the duke's overriding concern with his stomach, but his seems unlikely. Confucius's morality may have been revolutionary, but politically he remained a dyed-in-the-wool conservative. This is hardly surprising, considering the political anarchy and misery he saw around him. In such times it's not just the old fogeys who feel the need for "strong government, just like the good old days." To Confucius, the distant early years of the Chou dynasty appeared like a golden era. These had been times of firm government, cultural achievement, and stability, with the emperor ruling over his feudal lords. By Confucius's time this feudal system was beginning to break up, the feudal lords turning into feuding warlords. In his eyes, the alternative to a stratified society was anarchy.

Yet for Confucius the fundamental element of a moral society was not class, it was love. Here it's worth comparing Confucianism and Christianity. Both subscribed to the fundamental credo of "love one another." But Confucius was daring (or optimistic) enough to suggest that this could extend beyond the personal to society at large. Christianity drew short of prescribing for the state: "Render unto Caesar that which is Caesar's." Christianity was to succeed as the "slave morality" of a vicious empire, placing great emphasis on the individual and his salvation as well as a selfless love for others within the religion. Centuries later such ideas would transmogrify into Marxism—though for the most part government in the Christian West would remain pragmatic rather than principled. Confucianism, in adopting traditional Chinese virtues and pledging itself to a public morality, became synonymous with the Chinese way of life. Through the ages its exemplary morality and love for one's neighbor would only very gradually evolve, much like China itself. And despite all fervent denials, elements of Confucianism would still be recognizable in Maoist Marxism. Yet even as Marxism ebbs, the link between the Chinese self-image and government remains as strong as ever. As China begins to absorb Western ideas, the understanding of such

32

cultural similarities and differences will become increasingly important.

Confucius deals specifically with his political philosophy in the thirteenth book of his sayings. This starts with some basic no-nonsense advice: "Tzu-lu asked about government. The Master said: 'Encourage people to work hard by setting an example.'

"Tzu-lu asked what more he should do. The Master replied: 'Never slacken your efforts.'"

When he was asked how to run government, Confucius replied: "Show leniency towards minor mistakes, and promote men of talent."

"But how does one recognize men of talent?"

The Master said: "Promote those you your-self recognize. Those whom you do not recognize will come through of their own accord."

But the Master soon transcends such banalities. When asked the first thing he would do if he were put in charge of the government, Confucius replied: "First of all I would make sure that everything was named correctly."

"Really? Isn't that a little obtuse?"

"What an ignorant clod you are! When you

can't speak about something, you should remain silent." Having admonished his unfortunate disciple, Confucius went on to outline his linguistic theory of government: "If the names are not correct, language is without an object. When language has no object, nothing can be done properly. When nothing is done properly, the rituals fall into disarray, music becomes discordant, and punishments no longer fit the crime. When the punishment no longer fits the crime, no one knows where they are. Therefore, whatever one conceives of, one must be able to put into communicable speech. And whatever one says, one must be able to do. Where language is concerned, precision is of the utmost importance. Nothing must be left open to chance misinterpretation." This is all very well—but as your *first priority*? Indeed, one may wonder what all this has to do with government. (For centuries, incomprehensible directives have been an integral part of government.)

Confucius persists with this approach in regard to his next topic. Asked about the practice of agriculture, he offers a lengthy reply which has nothing to do with agriculture. "Fan Chi asked Confucius to teach him how to grow crops. The Master replied: 'I am not as good as an old farmer.' He then asked to be taught how to grow vegetables. Confucius replied: 'I am not as good as an old gardener.'"

When Fan Chi left, the Master exclaimed: "What an ignorant clod he is! When their superiors devote themselves to the rituals, none of the common people will dare to be irreverent. When they devote themselves to justice, none will dare to be disobedient. When they devote themselves to trustworthiness, none will dare to be insincere. Where such things are practiced, people will flock from far and wide with their babies strapped to their backs. What's the point in talking about growing crops?"

Confucius then appears to take a contrary stance. Having disparaged practical ability, he now points out its superiority over refinement: "Consider a man who can recite all three hundred poems in the traditional *Book of Songs*. You give him an official post, but he turns out to be incompetent. You send him abroad on a diplomatic mission, but he proves incapable of using his initiative. What use are all those poems, no matter how many he has learned?" The cultivation imparted by poetry is no different from the cultivation of turnips—both are equally useless in the cultivation of *jen*. When someone possesses this quality, all else follows. "If a ruler himself is upright in his own person then there will be obedience without orders having to be given; but if he himself is not upright, there will not be obedience even if orders are given."

Like so much of Confucius, this is laudable—but in practice sheer fantasy. Human nature being what it is, people obey a bloodthirsty tyrant with much more alacrity than they do an upright and humane ruler with good intentions. Why then is such advice laudable? Because Confucius was trying to improve the behavior of the abominable and unscrupulous rulers of his time. Any attempt to improve matters deserves commendation. But in choosing this course, Confucius limits the relevance of his advice to a particular time and a particular place.

All political advice suffers to a degree from this defect. The more pertinent it is, the quicker it becomes redundant. We only have to compare Confucius's political advice with that other great work of political instruction, Machiavelli's *The Prince*. Confucius's political wish fulfillment would have been irrelevant in Renaissance Italy, many of whose rulers were great believers in inspiring their people with cultured and exemplary behavior. Machiavelli's writing was intended to open the eyes of a ruler to political reality: bad behavior wins every time. By the same token, *The Prince* would have been redundant in the hands of any Chinese warlord of the late Chou dynasty. Such unscrupulous opportunism and vicious untrustworthiness were second nature there: essential requirements for any Chou ruler who wished to retain his job. Confucius was merely attempting to rectify the balance in favor of a more civilized outlook.

Central to Confucius's achievement was his ability as an educator. The main purpose of his school was to produce civil servants who could propagate his social and political ideas—the cultivation of human behavior and a compassionate society. He always stressed that the achievement of *jen* was not for the benefit of the individual but for society as a whole. "He cultivates himself so that he can bring peace and happiness to all the people." These new administrators were expected to see their work as a vocation rather than merely a means to advancement and self-aggrandizement. "It is shameful to make salary your whole object." The upright man should not be worried about poverty.

Despite his respect for the class system in politics, Confucius had no truck with it in his school. He believed in "education for all regardless of their class." At this time education was confined to the upper classes, so his open-door policy provided an exceptional opportunity for many who would otherwise have spent a life of drudgery and humiliation. As a result, most of Confucius's pupils came from lower-class backgrounds—and were to remain loyal and grateful to their master throughout their lives. In this way, Confucius was responsible for an injection of new talent as well as new ideas into the civil service of his region. He was well aware of what he was doing. "Where there is education, there are no class distinctions." (Sadly, in our eyes this again is bound to appear as laudable fantasy.)

Yet despite this covert egalitarianism, Confucius retained certain prejudices. "It is wrong for a gentleman to have knowledge of menial matters and proper that he should be entrusted with great responsibilities. It is wrong for a small man to be entrusted with great responsibilities, but proper that he should have a knowledge of menial matters."

Confucius was an excellent teacher, and many of his pupils went on to become highly successful administrators (somewhat to the chagrin of their aging master, who continued scouring the help-wanted scrolls without success). Wisely, Confucius's pupils would set aside many of his more unworkable principles as soon as they entered the real world of government. Advocating humane and revolutionary ideas would only have helped them to get a job in the boys' choir. Yet this first Confucian generation of ably educated administrators didn't forget their great teacher and what he had taught them. They formed a kind of masonic fraternity, and their education certainly affected the way they continued to live as well as their attitude toward their work. The first seeds of a new enlightenment were being sown. From now on, few seriously believed that their rulers were descended from divine ancestors, ruling by heavenly decree. It was understood that the state could indeed become a cooperative undertaking of the benefit of all; and the new administrators did their best to dissuade their masters from embarking upon senseless wars.

Among Confucius's pupils were a number of scions from influential families, usually from other provinces. But eventually a few curious members of the ruling family of Lu began to turn up at his lectures. In this way Confucius met the future ruling prince of Lu, Yang Hou (not to be confused with his notorious predecessor Yang Hoo, who became an object of derision [haha] after his regime turned into an increasing hooha). Yang Hou was impressed by Confucius, and when he took power he appointed the middle-aged philosopher minister of crime. At last Confucius could put his principles into practice.

According to all reports, Confucius was a huge success as minister of crime, though this seems to have had little to do with his much-vaunted principles. Confucius conducted a reign of terror against local criminals. "So long as he was in office there were no robbers in the land of Lu," writes his biographer H. G. Creel. Confucius even went so far as to establish the death penalty for "inventing unusual clothing"; and soon things became so orderly throughout the province that "the men were careful to walk on the right of the road, the women on the left." Eventually it was decided that enough was enough. Someone offered the chief minister a bribe of eighty beautiful young girls to get rid of Confucius. The chief minister, who had not had the benefit of a Confucian education, found himself unable to refuse this exhaustively challenging offer. Confucius was relieved of his post; the men and women of Lu reverted to walking on the same pavement, and began wearing fashionable clothes they wouldn't be seen dead in; and criminals were able to retire from unsuitable employment in order to follow their true calling.

In recognition of his services, Confucius was offered promotion to an even more prestigious post with a highly impressive title and salary. But he quickly discovered that this was a mere sinecure, with no authority whatsoever. He resigned at once in disgust. He wasn't interested in the job if he didn't have the power to decide important matters of state.

Confucius was now over fifty years old. He decided to set out, accompanied by a few disciples, on a pilgrimage around China. But this was not a pilgrimage in the usual spiritual sense. It had no holy destination, and Confucius wasn't seeking enlightenment on the way. His pilgrimage, like his philosophy, had wholly secular intentions. He was looking for a job. And if he couldn't find a job, perhaps he could find a future ruler whom he could tutor, so that at last somewhere his principles could be put into practice. But word had obviously spread about Confucius. His pilgrimage in search of the holy grail of employment was to last more than ten years. Occasionally he would be asked for advice, but once again no offers of a permanent job progressed beyond the interview stage.

We can only speculate about the reasons for this. Confucius was now generally regarded as the wisest man throughout China. He had taught many of its most able administrators; and he had even held minor office himself, without accepting a single bribe or even betraying his master to his enemies. (Such eccentricity was considered almost perverse and certainly contributed to the later belief that Confucius was a purely legendary character who had never existed.) There was obviously something about Confucius. Earnestness, unwillingness to compromise, unpleasant personal habits, or perhaps just simple halitosis of the soul—we shall never know precisely what it was about him that didn't appeal to the Chinese ruling classes. My own opinion, after studying his writings, is that they may just have found him a colossal bore.

Even Confucius's adventures during his decade of travels seem to have acquired this characteristic element of boringness. When he visited the state of Wei he had a private audience with the ruler's sister, the notorious Nan Tzu, which deeply upset his disciples. But history has prudishly censored whatever it was that so upset Confucius's disciples, and we don't even learn how Nan Tzu achieved her celebrated notoriety, apart from some trivial gossip about royal incest. In the province of Sung, Confucius learned that someone was out to assassinate him, so he took to wearing "inconspicuous clothing." And so his prosaic pilgrimage continued. In Sung he is also said to have met the local ruler and talked long into the night with him, eventually convincing his host that his ideas on how to rule were worth following. Virtue and competent administration, not personal ambition, were the keys to success. Confucius's crusade had made another conquest. Boredom had once again defeated barbarism. But even this ruler curmudgeonly refused to offer Confucius a job.

By now Confucius was sixty-seven. His lesser coevals were all happily retired, but he was still trying to get his career started. In the end, Confucius's disciples back in Lu decided that the only answer was to invite their master home again. It was time for this most practical of philosophers, who all his life had preached the virtues of an honest day's work, to abandon forever the idea that he would be able to earn a living. Confucius duly returned home and lived out his last five years in Lu. These were sad years. His favorite disciple, Yen Hui, died and for once in his life Confucius lapsed briefly into despair. "Alas, there is no one who understands me," he told his remaining disciples. He became convinced that his vital message would never reach the generations to come. His son Lieu also died. Practically nothing is known of Lieu's life. He is said to have exhibited no exceptional qualities, but later evidence points against this. Within just a few centuries there were more than forty thousand people in China who claimed to be descended from Confucius—which would seem to indicate exceptional activity by the master's only son.

Confucius spent his last years reading, editing, and writing commentaries on the Chinese classics, the canon of works dating from the period when China emerged from antiquity. (The *Lun Yu—The Sayings of Confucius*—were to be added to this canon before it was carved in stone in the mid-third century B.C.) The Chinese classics ranged from the sublime *Shih* (*Poems*, sometimes known as the *Book of Songs*), which incorporate legendary material with timeless day-to-day details of earliest Chinese life, to the mysterious and much misused *I Ching* (*Book of Changes*), an intriguing blend of metaphysical mumbo jumbo and psychological insight. The latter began life as a book of divination. Like Babylonian astrology, which dates from this same period of humanity's adolescence, it contains an edifice of gnomic wisdom built on the flimsiest of foundations.

The *I Ching*'s undeniably esoteric nature is an embarrassment to Confucian scholars, who rightly insist upon the master's strictly down-to-earth approach to philosophy. Yet there is no denying that Confucius spent many years of his life reading this book, and during his last years in Lu wrote an extensive commentary upon it.

Far from pooh-poohing the *I Ching*'s often fantastic contents, this commentary even includes instructions about how to use the work for divination purposes by throwing little sticks in the air and reading the patterns they form. On the face of it, this seems as likely as discovering that Hegel was a closet ballet dancer—but even philosophers must have their hobbies, and throwing little sticks in the air to find out who's going to win the 2:30 race at Shanghai seems harmless enough to me.

Confucius also spent his last years passing on the fundamentals of his philosophy to his disciples. As should be clear by now, this wasn't really a philosophy at all—not in the Western sense of the word. Confucius's teachings do contain references to epistemology, logic, metaphysics, and aesthetics—the traditional categories of philosophy—but they are only passing references and form no system. Confucius's teachings also pass comment on the taste for ginger and the length of nightgowns, without containing a comprehensive cuisine or theory of fashion. But judging from Confucius's period as minister of crime it seems likely that he did have a very definite theory of fashion. So he might well have formulated comprehensive theories of cuisine and philosophy that have not come down to us.

This Confucian learning and spiritual instruction was to form the basic education of the mandarin class which ran the Chinese administration for more than two millennia. Like all such hierarchies, it eventually ossified. Confucius had foreseen the need to adapt to the times. "The only ones who do not change are sages and idiots." But Confucius's warning was to no avail. Perhaps it is the fate of all civil services to be run by sages and idiots.

In 479 B.C., at the age of seventy-two, Confucius lay on his deathbed. His disciples kept watch over him during his final illness. His last words were recorded by his favored pupil Tze-Lu:

"The great mountain must crumble,
The strong beam bursts,
The wise man must wither away like a plant."

48

Confucius was buried by his disciples in the city of Ch'ufou by the Ssu River. The temple built on this site and the surrounding precincts were preserved as holy. For more than two thousand years this site was visited by a continuous stream of pilgrims. The recent hiatus in this tradition during the Communist era is now apparently over—the end of a brief lapse in a venerable Chinese tradition established long before the birth of Socrates and Christ.

Judging from Confucius's last words, he was well aware of his greatness but uncertain that his message would long survive him. Confucius was quite right to be worried on this score. Confucianism may have survived for nearly two and a half millennia, but its resemblance to the original teachings of Confucius himself has sometimes been difficult to detect (much as it is difficult to relate the Inquisition and the burning of heretics to the message of the figure who delivered the Sermon on the Mount). But Confucius's message was not completely subverted by his followers. Just over two centuries after his death, the Han dynasty established the first great age of Chinese culture. This dynasty was for the most part run according to Confucian principles, which proved so successful that the dynasty thrived for more than four hundred years, outlasting most other Chinese empires and setting a cultural example which successive dynasties strove to emulate. In the West, Confucius was to be admired by Leibniz and his contemporary rationalist Voltaire, who declared: "I respect Confucius. He was the first man who did *not* receive divine inspiration."

A trivial echo of Confucius's teaching is today found in the martial art of kung fu, which is named after the master (Kungfutzu) but bears as much resemblance to its nominal origin as a Mars bar does to the planet. Similarly debased echoes of Confucius may be detected in the aberration in Chinese thinking that recently supplanted the teachings of the master. The personality cult of President Mao, the pilgrimage of the Communists' Long March, and the veneration of the Little Red Book (containing the "Sayings of Chairman Mao") bear an unmistakable resemblance to the cult that grew up around

Confucius (which resulted in his portrait hanging in every classroom throughout China), his own long pilgrimage in search of a political job, and the veneration of the classic *Sayings of Confucius*. But all this probably wouldn't have bothered Confucius much. As he remarked, "I am different. I take life as it comes."

Afterword: Chinese Philosophy

It's been said that the West has never really understood Chinese philosophy. Indeed, many oriental thinkers claim it is impossible for the Western mind to grasp such subtleties of which it has no conception.

Almost all Western philosophers have maintained a similar view—usually regarding the reception by Western civilization of their own philosophy. So we should not be unduly put off by this insistence on mutual incomprehension. Chinese philosophy *is* different from Western philosophy, just as the Chinese are different from Europeans. But we are all equally worthless, or precious, *sub specie aeterni* (beneath the gaze of eternity). We all inhabit the same human condition, and this is what every philosophy claims to examine. So Chinese philosophy may have its inadequacies in our eyes as ours may have in theirs—but they are both prescriptions for a similar complaint: life.

Chinese philosophy as such came into being from the sixth century B.C. onward. During this period there developed the Hundred Schools, which were as diverse and divergent as their name suggests. These consisted largely of wandering philosophers who traveled among the different states that then made up China. Upon arrival the philosopher would set up shop and begin giving philosophical advice of one sort or another. This was usually given to the court and frequently consisted of various principles intended to help with the government of the state. Inevitably such advice was seldom tolerated for long, and the philosopher soon found himself back on the road.

The philosophies produced by the Hundred Schools were often unrecognizable as philosophy, according to the Western notion of this subject. Frequently these philosophies were little more than an "attitude to life," elaborated in a number of pithy or enigmatic sayings. Their actual philosophy was seldom structured or argued in any consistent, logical manner, and was often closer to political advice on the one hand, or religion on the other.

The main example of the former was Confucianism, and the latter Taoism. These soon emerged as the two dominant strains of thought in Chinese philosophy. Later they were both to be affected by the arrival of the third main strain in Chinese philosophy: Buddhism.

Confucianism

The teachings that originated with Confucius have lasted in one form or another to this day. Confucianism is essentially practical. It is concerned with how to live on the personal and social levels. For this reason its main topics are ethics and politics. There is little speculation about the meaning and ultimate nature of life. Metaphysics is for the most part absent. This has been true of Confucianism since its beginning more than two and a half millennia ago, and continues to be true of Neo-Confucianism in its present diffuse form.

Confucianism has shown that it is possible to conduct one's life without recourse to metaphysical speculation. After 2,500 years Western thinking appears, reluctantly and very gradually, to be coming round to the same point of view.

Taoism

Taoism springs from the Chinese word *tao*, which means "the Way." All Chinese philosophers had their views about *tao*, but Taoism itself derived from those held by the sage Lao-tzu and his later follower, Chuang-tzu. Lao-tzu lived during the sixth century B.C., but little is known of his life. He is said to have been a historian and religious adviser at the court of the Chou emperors. According to legend, he met Confucius and was not impressed. Later he is said to have set off for the West. At the Hsien-ku Pass, the guardian of the pass refused to allow him to leave China until he had written down his teachings about the *tao*. This book was named the *Tao-te Ching* and was to become the holy writ of Taoism. Lao-tzu then departed for the West, and, according to a contemporary report, "nobody knows what has become of him." Many among the Hundred Schools looked upon Lao-tzu as a sage, a saint, or even a deity. Even contemporary Confucians are said to have regarded him as a great philosopher. This is difficult to understand, as the teachings of Lao-tzu are complementary to those of Confucius. In the view of some, these two philosophies deal with entirely different realms of human endeavor; in the view of others, they are utterly contradictory on almost every issue.

Where Confucius taught the "Way of Man," Lao-tzu taught the "Way of Nature." For Lao-tzu, the Way was a largely metaphysical, mystical conception. It was the eternal and absolute force that controls nature, but it remains beyond space and time. This is difficult to grasp in the logical conceptual terms normally required of philosophical discourse by Western thinkers. Yet it is not, as is sometimes claimed, extraneous to philosophy as we know it in the West. Stoicism, and the philosophy advocated by the Cynics, were likewise fundamentally attitudes toward the world.

According to Lao-tzu, we should attune ourselves to the *tao* by attempting to emulate it. We should empty ourselves of petty concerns, dedicate our lives to simplicity and spontaneity, yet at the same time remain tranquil.

When conveyed by an exemplary teacher such as Lao-tzu, Taoism doubtless had great force. But a certain amount of elaboration was needed if Taoism was to remain viable even as a metaphysical philosophy. This was provided by Chuang-tzu, who was born a couple of centuries after Lao-tzu. Again, little is known of his life except that he wrote the book which is now named after him, the *Chuang-tzu*, and that he vehemently attacked Confucianism. In his later years he is said to have become a delightful old eccentric—dressed in rags, with his disintegrating shoes held together by bits of string. One of his disciples visited Chuang-tzu after his wife had died, and was disconcerted to find him happily singing away to himself and beating time on his bowl. Chuang-tzu defended his behavior by saying that to weep and mourn would have been to display an "ignorance of destiny."

For Chuang-tzu, the *tao* transforms haphazard and conflicting nature into the harmonious unity of the Way of Nature. This happens only when nature follows Nature, and is achieved by us when we too follow the Way of Nature— rather than the Way of Man, as recommended by Confucius. The *tao* (or Way of Nature) is a transcendent state where good and evil no longer exist, and all things live in harmonious equality. But Chuang-tzu also maintained that the *tao* was everywhere and existed in all things, even down to ants and excrement. On his deathbed he forbad his pupils from giving him any kind of formal funeral, saying he preferred to be left so that he could be eaten by carrion crows rather than buried and eaten by worms.

Buddhism

Buddhism arrived in China in the third century A.D. from India. During its long period of development away from the country of its origin,

Buddhism underwent a peculiarly Chinese transformation which owes much to its numerous similarities to Taoism.

Buddhism is considered by Westerners as more of a religion than a philosophy. But one has only to look at Scholasticism in the Middle Ages to see how these two essentially separate modes of thought can become inextricably entwined. Regarded in this light, Buddhism is certainly a philosophy as well as a religion, its metaphysics being quite the equal of Scholasticism (or Taoism, for that matter). Unlike the Scholastics, however, the Buddhists tended to believe in a laissez-faire fatalism, especially with regard to schisms. As a result, it wasn't long before Buddhism diverged into a wide variety of religio-philosophies. These all insisted upon calling themselves Buddhism, despite the fact that many of them were inimical to one another. (The parallels with Christian thought are again all too evident, with the difference that in such times of difficulty Buddhists prefer to set fire to themselves rather than each other.)

Buddhism was founded by Siddhartha Gautama, who was born in Nepal in the mid-sixth century B.C. After getting married at sixteen and living a life of luxury for another thirteen years, he abandoned everything and set off for India, where he became a vagabond ascetic. In danger of wasting away through his overzealous approach to asceticism, he eventually decided to follow his own path to enlightenment. According to legend he finally achieved this enlightenment around 528 B.C., at the age of thirty-five, and thus became Buddha. This happened while he was meditating cross-legged beneath a Banyan or East Indian Fig Tree (*Ficus religiosa*).

Initially Buddhism placed great emphasis on meditation, which gave one sufficient spiritual tranquility and detachment to free oneself from the delusions and contradictions of life in the everyday world. These daily snares are like clouds obscuring the sun; only when they are dissolved by spiritual discipline do we become aware of the radiant truth.

Chinese Buddhism was greatly influenced by Taoism, which was prevalent in China at the time of Buddhism's arrival. Later Buddhism was to have its own influence over the development of Confucianism in the eleventh century. This Neo-Confucianism absorbed from Buddhism metaphysical concerns which would have been anathema to Confucius himself but appeared to fill a gap in his teachings for his followers.

The Sayings of Confucius

Confucius's advice on how to be a good administrator, and the effect of this:

Chuansun Shih asked the Master: "What must I do to become a superior man and enter government service?"

"You must respect the five high qualities and abhor the four evils."

"What are these five high qualities?"

"The superior man is gracious without accepting bribes. He works alongside people without giving cause for resentment. He has ambitions, but he is not avaricious. He is dignified, but without undue pride. He inspires respect, but is not cruel."

"What precisely do you mean by these qualities?"

"To work for the advantage of the people, isn't this being generous without accepting bribes? If you give the right job to the right person, who will be resentful? If a man, out of desire to fulfil himself, achieves all he is capable of—how can he be greedy? The superior man always takes on his tasks regardless of their difficulty or size, and thus is not slothful—this surely is dignity without pride? The superior man takes care about his appearance. He wears his clothes and hat in the proper manner, and treats others with respect. And owing to his serious demeanor, people have great regard for him—in this way he inspires respect without being cruel."

"And what are the four evils?"

"To put a man to death because he failed in his task when he wasn't given the proper instructions—this is cruelty. To expect a man to do something without the proper advice—this is an outrage. To insist that a man rushes to complete his task, when he has been told to perform it thoroughly—this is detrimental. To promise a reward and then begrudge paying it—this is small-mindedness."

—Sayings of Confucius

A few more tips for good government:
"If a ruler himself is upright in his own person, then there will be obedience without orders having to be given; but if he himself is not upright, there will not be obedience even if orders are given."

"If only some ruler would employ me, I'd have everything sorted out within a month. And within three years I would have the whole place running smoothly."

Speaking of government, the Master told Chung Yu: "Only ask others to do what you have first taught them."

—Sayings of Confucius

Confucius emphasizes the need for study and comments on our general attitude toward it:
"Study as if you will never learn, as if you were afraid of losing what you wish to learn."

"It is difficult to find a man who is willing to study for three years without getting a job at the end of it."

—Sayings of Confucius

Some penetrating observations by the great Master:
"Don't anticipate fraud or deceitfulness, but at the same time always be on the lookout for them—this is necessary if you wish to get to the top."

"Someone who is keen on bravery but complains of being poor is going to create trouble."

"Some people can be made to do things without being able to understand them."

—Sayings of Confucius

Some not so penetrating observations by the great Master:
"When the weather becomes cold, we notice that the pines and firs are the last to fade."

When asked for further advice on government, the Master replied: "Never grow weary."

The Master said of Kungtzuching of Wei: "He knows how to enjoy things. When he first became successful he would say: 'This is just about right.' When he became a bit more successful, he would say: 'This is just about enough.' And when he became highly successful he would say: 'This is just about perfect.'"

—*Sayings of Confucius*

Confucius's celebrated description of himself and the stages of his life:
"When I was fifteen I was only interested in studying; when I was thirty I began my life; at forty I was self-assured; at fifty I understood my place in the vast scheme of things; at sixty I

learned to give up arguing; and now at seventy I can do whatever I like without disrupting my life."

—Sayings of Confucius

A court official asked Confucius if the lord Chao always obeyed the rites and observances, and Confucius replied that he did.

When Confucius left, the official said: "I was told that the great master Confucius was a wise man, but I can see that he is not. The lord Chao contravened the observances by taking a wife from amongst his own family, and disguised this fact by giving her a different name."

When Confucius was told of this, he replied: "When *I* make a mistake, you can be sure that everyone will get to hear about it."

—Sayings of Confucius

A typical example of the Master's pragmatism, wisdom, and advice about life:
"Be of unwavering good faith, love learning, be prepared to defend the good Way with your life.

Do not enter a state that is unstable; never live in a state where there is revolution. Strive to shine when the Way prevails in the Empire; when it does not prevail, then hide. It is shameful to be poor and unknown in a country where the Way prevails. Likewise, it is shameful to be rich and honored in a country where the Way does not prevail."

—*Sayings of Confucius*

The nearest Confucius comes to revealing a definitive theory of fashion:
"The superior man should not wear a crimson- or plum-colored collar on his clothes. The garments that he wears when he is indoors should not be colored scarlet or violet. In summer he should wear about the house a single gown made of rough or fine hemp. When he goes outside he should at all times put on a gown. In winter he should wear a black outer gown over a wool-lined garment. When wearing an undyed gown, his inner garment should be lined with deerskin. When wearing his yellow gown, his

inner garment should be lined with fox fur. When he is at home he should wear a lined gown that is longer than the one he wears for ceremonial occasions. This should have a short right sleeve, so that he can use his arm. When going to bed he must always wear a nightshirt, which should be half as long again as his body. At home his gowns should be lined with fox or badger fur. He should always wear all his badges of office hanging from his sash, except at funerals. His clothes must always be well tailored, apart from when he attends sacrifices. When visiting someone in mourning he should never wear a gown lined with wool or a black hat. On the first day of the month he should visit his prince dressed in formal wear. When he is undertaking a fast, he should at all times wear clean hempen robes."

—*Sayings of Confucius*

Some commentators have considered this advice to be so detailed that it does in fact constitute a genuine theory of fashion. My own view is that this is not the case, owing to its lack of abstract principles and certain inherent contradictions which remain unresolved. What, for instance, should the superior man wear if he is attending a sacrifice in the company of his prince on the first day of the month?

Some Western comments:
"I respect Confucius. He was the first man who did *not* receive divine inspiration."

—Voltaire

"What he transmitted was the values which the Chinese people for ages before him had cherished. So it's not so much that China is Confucian, as that Confucianism is Chinese."

—William McNaughton

"If we have to choose one word to characterize Confucian ethics, that word would have to be humanity. The main concern of Confucian ethics is the whole process of learning to be human. This process involves a total commitment, a continuous effort of self-refinement or self-

improvement and a holistic vision of the entire
project of moral education."

—Dr. Tu Wei-ming, Professor of Chinese
History and Philosophy, Harvard University

Confucius was more concerned with "the neces-
sities of government and of government administration than any other philosopher."

—Ezra Pound

Chronology of Significant Philosophical Dates

6th C B.C.	The beginning of Western philosophy with Thales of Miletus.
End of 6th C B.C.	Death of Pythagoras.
399 B.C.	Socrates sentenced to death in Athens.
c 387 B.C.	Plato founds the Academy in Athens, the first university.
335 B.C.	Aristotle founds the Lyceum in Athens, a rival school to the Academy.

324 A.D.	Emperor Constantine moves capital of Roman Empire to Byzantium.
400 A.D.	St. Augustine writes his *Confessions*. Philosophy absorbed into Christian theology.
410 A.D.	Sack of Rome by Visigoths heralds opening of Dark Ages.
529 A.D.	Closure of Academy in Athens by Emperor Justinian marks end of Hellenic thought.
Mid-13th C	Thomas Aquinas writes his commentaries on Aristotle. Era of Scholasticism.
1453	Fall of Byzantium to Turks, end of Byzantine Empire.
1492	Columbus reaches America. Renaissance in Florence and revival of interest in Greek learning.
1543	Copernicus publishes *On the Revolution of the Celestial Orbs*, proving mathematically that the earth revolves around the sun.

1633	Galileo forced by church to recant heliocentric theory of the universe.
1641	Descartes publishes his *Meditations*, the start of modern philosophy.
1677	Death of Spinoza allows publication of his *Ethics*.
1687	Newton publishes *Principia*, introducing concept of gravity.
1689	Locke publishes *Essay Concerning Human Understanding*. Start of empiricism.
1710	Berkeley publishes *Principles of Human Knowledge*, advancing empiricism to new extremes.
1716	Death of Leibniz.
1739–1740	Hume publishes *Treatise of Human Nature*, taking empiricism to its logical limits.
1781	Kant, awakened from his "dogmatic slumbers" by Hume, publishes *Critique of Pure Reason*.

Great era of German metaphysics begins.

1807   Hegel publishes *The Phenomenology of Mind*, high point of German metaphysics.

1818   Schopenhauer publishes *The World as Will and Representation*, introducing Indian philosophy into German metaphysics.

1889   Nietzsche, having declared "God is dead," succumbs to madness in Turin.

1921   Wittgenstein publishes *Tractatus Logico-Philosophicus*, claiming the "final solution" to the problems of philosophy.

1920s   Vienna Circle propounds Logical Positivism.

1927   Heidegger publishes *Being and Time*, heralding split between analytical and Continental philosophy.

1943   Sartre publishes *Being and Nothingness*, advancing

Heidegger's thought and instigating existentialism.

1953   Posthumous publication of Wittgenstein's *Philosophical Investigations*. High era of linguistic analysis.

Chronology of Confucius's Life

551 B.C.	Birth of Confucius (possibly on September 28, which is still celebrated as his birthday in parts of East Asia).
548 B.C.	Death of Confucius's father.
536 B.C.	Becomes obsessed with learning.
533 B.C.	Marries Peiu.
c 520–510 B.C.	Sets up school teaching his new "religion."
c 590–500 B.C.	Appointed minister of crime in province of Lu.
c 500 B.C.	Resigns from public office in province of Lu.

c 500–490 B.C.	Sets off on pilgrimage, looking for further employment.
484 B.C.	Returns home to province of Lu.
479 B.C.	Death of Confucius at age seventy-three.

Recommended Reading

Confucius, *The Analects*, trans. by Arthur Waley (Vintage Books, 1989). Good clear translation with useful introduction.

H. G. Creel, *Confucius and the Chinese Way* (Harper & Row, 1975). The best modern Western biography.

Raymond Stanley Dawson, *Confucius* (Oxford University Press, 1992). A useful introduction to the full range of Confucius's thought.

Hans Gerth and Max M. Weber, *The Religion of China: Confucianism and Taoism* (Free Press, 1968).

Tu Wei-ming, ed., *Confucian Ethics Today* (Federal, 1984). A series of papers and discussions about the practical application of Confucianism in the modern world, especially in regard to the Singapore experiment (the squeaky-clean ministate has introduced a strict version of Confucianism as state practice).

Index

A NOTE ON THE AUTHOR

Paul Strathern has lectured in philosophy and mathematics and now lives and writes in London. A Somerset Maugham prize winner, he is also the author of books on history and travel as well as five novels. His articles have appeared in a great many publications, including the *Observer* (London) and the *Irish Times*. His own degree in philosophy was earned at Trinity College, Dublin.